Theater for children
created by children

By **Maru García**

To my Dad for the best advice ever which encourage me to follow my dreams: "El que es perico donde quiera es verde."

"Acting is in everything but the words."

— Stella Adler, The Art of Acting

"Imagination is the beginning of creation. You imagine what you desire, you will what you imagine, and at last, you create what you will"
– George Bernard Shaw

"Creativity is an area in which younger people have a tremendous advantage, since they have an endearing habit of always questioning past wisdom and authority."
-Bill Hewlett

Table of contents

Introduction

As any artistic activity, drama supports the growth and development of the children by helping them expand their creativity while encouraging their self-expression. Drama, theater, and story-acting encourage children to create fictional spaces where they can communicate with one another, express themselves, and use their imagination.

With some guidance, children are able to create fascinating stories in which they use their imagination and apply their understanding of the world to their work on stage. Even very young children are able to express themselves through dramatic play. When they create imaginary worlds, they are able to work through their anxieties and fears as well as express their joy and contentment.

In 2014 I had the opportunity to teach drama at a charter school in Denver. The objective was to involve the students in a creative adventure in which they could explore the wonderful world of theater. Students of all ages were involved in the process of inventing the story, creating the dialogues, rehearsing and presenting it to their parents and teachers.

The process with each one of the groups started with some guided improvisations in which the children explored different characters. Throughout the first two week with each one of the groups, the students were asked to sketch the basic story and create some dialogues. At the same time, each one of them chose a character that could fit in the story. After the dialogues were created, I put them together in a script format. The rest of the time was spent rehearsing and memorizing. One of the groups even created their own set. The result was amazing.

The children felt proud and excited about the opportunity of recreating a character they had just invented a few months before the performance. The stories are simple and direct albeit charming and imaginative. The results always surprised me. These are the stories the children wrote and created.

Presentation

This is a scary story.
A story to make you shiver.
A story to make you scream.
Most of us like scary stories
Because we like feeling scared
When there is no real danger
Feeling scared is fun.
Ghosts, Zombies, Mummies
Boys, Girls, Talking Cats
This is a story we created
And that we gladly present.

The Big Treasure

by Kindergarten Students

Characters:

Narrator (an adult)

Ladybugs

Caterpillars

Butterflies

Dragons

Dinosaurs

Narrator:	Once up a time. There were three caterpillars and three ladybugs that wanted to find the treasure of the magic mountain.
Ladybugs:	We want to find the treasure.
Caterpillars:	We want to find the treasure too.
Ladybugs:	Let's go together.
Caterpillars:	That is a great idea.
Narrator:	So they started walking through the forest. They had to be careful not to step on the pinecones. Sometimes it was dark and they got a little scared.
Ladybugs:	It is too dark.
Caterpillars:	We are scared.
Narrator:	But they continued walking because they really wanted the treasure. After the forest they found a desert.
Ladybugs:	The desert is huge.
Caterpillars:	But we have to go through it.
Narrator:	So they walked through the desert to get to the treasure. They walked for many days until they couldn't walk any more.
Ladybugs:	We cannot walk any more.
Caterpillars:	We can't either.
Ladybugs:	We are thirsty.
Caterpillars:	And tired.
Narrator:	They were so tired, they fainted. That day in the afternoon, two butterflies flew by and saw them.

Butterflies:	Do you see that? I think they are our friends. Let's get them water.
Narrator:	So the butterflies went to the river and brought water for them.
Ladybugs:	Thank you butterflies.
Caterpillars:	Thank you, you saved us.
Butterflies:	Why are you here?
Ladybugs:	We are going to the magic mountain.
Caterpillars:	We want to find the treasure.
Butterflies:	Can we go with you?

Ladybugs & Caterpillars: Sure.

Narrator:	So they went together towards the magic mountain. They arrived to the edge of the magic mountain where they found two dragons.
Dragons:	Roar!!!

Ladybugs, Caterpillars, Butterflies: Ahhhh!

Caterpillars:	We are scared of you.
Dragons:	We are terrifying.
Ladybugs:	We are scared of you.
Dragons:	Go away! We don't want you here.
Butterflies:	We are not going away.
Dragons:	What are you doing here?
Ladybugs:	We are going to find the treasure.
Dragons:	What treasure?
Butterflies:	The treasure in the mountain.
Dragons:	Where?

Caterpillars:	At the top of the volcano.
Dragons:	You will never make it.
Butterflies:	Why not?
Dragons:	It is too far.
Ladybugs:	Can you take us there?
Dragons:	Sure. Climb on our backs.
Butterflies:	We will fly next to you.
Narrator:	The caterpillars and the ladybugs climbed on the dragons' backs. The butterflies flew next to them. It was difficult to hold on to the dragons.
Caterpillars:	Oh no, we are sliding down!
Butterflies:	We can help you get back up.
Caterpillars:	Thank you.
Dragons:	Hold on tight.
Narrator:	Finally they arrived to the magic mountain.
Dragons:	Here we are. You can get down now.
Ladybugs:	Follow us now.
Caterpillar:	Let's make a line.
Ladybugs:	We go first.
Caterpillars:	We go second.
Butterflies:	We go third.
Dragons:	And we go last.
Narrator:	They started climbing towards the volcano but all of a sudden they encountered two dinosaurs.
Dinosaurs:	Where are you going?
Ladybugs:	We are going to find the treasure.

Dinosaurs:	You cannot get the treasure.
Caterpillars:	Why not?
Dinosaurs:	We tried before but we could not get it.
Butterflies:	Let us go through.
Dinosaurs:	No, you cannot pass.
Dragons:	If you don't let us through we will have to fight.
Dinosaurs:	Oh really?
Dragons:	Yes, because you are not being nice to us.
Dinosaurs:	We don't have to be nice to you.
Dragons:	Yes you do.
Dinosaurs:	Why?
Dragons:	Because we are being nice to you.
Dinosaurs:	That is not a reason. Let's fight!
Ladybugs:	Stop!
Caterpillars:	Stop now!
Butterflies:	Stop please!
Dinosaurs:	What?
Ladybugs:	We can all go find the treasure together.
Caterpillars:	Together we can get it.
Butterflies:	Yes.
Dinosaurs:	Do you think that if we work together we can find it?
All: Yes.	
Dragons:	But you have to be nice to us.
Dinosaurs:	Fine. We will be nice.
Caterpillars:	We will climb on the dragons' back.
Ladybugs:	And we will climb on the dinosaurs' back.

Butterflies:	We will fly in front of you to guide you.
Narrator:	So all together climbed up to the volcano where the treasure was.
Dinosaurs:	There it is.
Dragons:	Look at all the gold.
Ladybugs:	And the necklaces.
Caterpillars:	How are we going to take it?
Butterflies:	We will put it in some bags and the dinosaurs and dragons can carry it.
Narrator:	So the ladybugs, the caterpillars, and the butterflies put in bags as many gold coins and jewels as they could.
Dinosaurs:	Great! Put the bags around our backs.
Dragons:	Put some others around us too.
Ladybugs:	Here you are.
Caterpillars:	We have to get out of here.
Butterflies:	The volcano is about to explode.
Dinosaurs:	Hurry, climb on our back too.
Dragons:	We can carry the ladybugs again.
Butterflies:	Great! Let's get away quickly.
Narrator:	So all together they got away from the magic mountain before the volcano exploded.
Dinosaurs:	Look back, the volcano is erupting.
Dragons:	Wow! That is a lot of lava.
Ladybugs:	We are glad we are not there anymore.
Caterpillars:	What should we do with the treasure?

Butterflies:	Each one of us should take a coin and we can bury the rest of it.
Dinosaurs:	That is a great idea.
Dragons:	We can make a hole with our tails.
Dinosaurs:	We can help.
Ladybugs:	Make a big, big hole.
Caterpillars:	A huge hole!
Narrator:	So the dragons and the dinosaurs make a hole so everyone can put the gold inside.
Ladybugs:	Let's put the gold inside.
Caterpillars:	Let's put the diamonds inside.
Butterflies:	Now let's cover the hole.
Dragons & Dinosaurs:	We can do that.
Ladybugs, Caterpillars, Butterflies:	We can help.
Narrator:	So all together they buried the treasure.
Dinosaurs:	Now what?
Dragon:	We think we can all be friends.
Ladybugs:	Yes, that is a great idea.
Caterpillars:	Maybe we can find more treasures.
Butterflies:	Yes!
Narrator:	The Dragons, the Dinosaurs, the Ladybugs, the Caterpillars, and the Butterflies became best friends. Together they found many, many more treasures.

THE END

A Haunted House

by 1st. Grade students

Characters:

Narrator

Princess

Cat

Ghosts

Werewolves

Vampires

Prince

Witch

Transformers

Ninja Turtles

Narrator: Once upon a time, a Princess and a Cat were playing hide and seek.

Princess: Cat, come here, let's play together.

Cat: What do you want to play?

Princess: I want to play hide and seek.

Cat: That sounds fun.

Princess: Great! I will count first.

Cat: I will hide.

Princess: Fine, I will count next to that tree over there. *(exits)*

Cat: Where should I hide?

(Some Ghosts come in)

Ghosts: Hi Cat, what are you doing?

Cat: I am playing hide and seek with the princess but I don't know where to hide.

Ghosts: Why don't you hide in our house?

Cat: What house?

Ghosts: That one, over there on top of the hill.

Cat: That is a great idea.

Ghosts: We will go with you.

Narrator: So the Cat went with the Ghosts to the House but he didn't know it was haunted.

Ghosts:	Welcome to our house.
Cat:	It is very big.
Ghosts:	We are the ghosts of the house.
Cat:	I am a Cat.
Ghosts:	Welcome, would you like some milk?
Cat:	Milk? I love milk.
Ghosts:	Let's go to the kitchen then. *(They exit)*
Narrator:	Mean while, the Princess was looking for the Cat.

(Princess enters)

Princess:	Cat, cat, where are you? Maybe he went to that house.
Narrator:	So the Princess went to the house.
Princess:	Cat, Cat, are you here?

(Werewolves enter)

Werewolves:	Who are you looking for?
Princess:	Ahhhh!
Werewolves:	Who are you looking for?
Princess:	My cat.
Werewolves:	We haven't seen him. And if we would, we would have eaten him.
Princess:	I know. Well, I will continue looking.
Werewolves:	Not so fast.

Princess: Why?

Werewolves: You look delicious, maybe we will eat you.

Princess: Me? Oh no! Princesses taste terrible.

(Vampires enter)

Vampires: We have sucked the blood of princesses before and it is
                delicious.

Princess: Oh, where did you come from?

Vampires: We flew.

Princess: Well, I am looking for my Cat.

Vampires: We know. But we don't think you will get out of here.

Princess: No please, let me go.

Vampires: Don't think so. Either we suck your blood or the
                werewolves may eat you.

(The Cat and the Ghosts come in)

Cat: Princess!

Princess: Cat!

Ghosts: Leave her alone!

Werewolves: Why?

Ghosts: She is the friend of the Cat. They are our guests.

Vampires: But we want her blood.

Ghosts: No! They are our friends.

Werewolves: Fine! But don't ask for any help later.

Ghosts: We won't.

(The Vampires and the Werewolves exit)

Princess: Thank you.

Cat: That was very brave of you.

Ghosts: Well, let's go finish our milk.

(The Princess, the Cat, the Ghosts and the Mummies leave. The Prince comes in)

Prince: Princess, Cat, are you here?

(The Witch comes in)

Witch: Yes, they are here.

Prince: Great! Where are they?

Witch: In the kitchen.

Prince: Take me there please.

Witch: Of course not.

Prince: What?

Witch: You are my prisoner.

Prince: Oh no!

Witch: Oh yes!

Prince: But why?

Witch: Because I want to control the kingdom.

Prince: But I am not the king.

Witch:	Not yet, but you will be…and when you are the kingdom will be mine!
Prince:	And the Princess?
Witch:	That is not a problem. The vampires and werewolves will finish her.
Prince:	I have friends, you know?
Witch:	Really, like who?
Prince:	You will see soon.
Witch:	Really?
Prince:	Yes, they are almost here.

(The Transformers and the Ninja Turtles come in)

Transformers:	Prince, we are here.
Ninja Turtles:	We came to rescue you.
Prince:	I told you.
Witch:	I have friends too. Vampires, werewolves come here!
Vampires:	We can help you.
Werewolves:	Let's take them down.
Prince:	Let's see who wins.

(They fight in slow motion. The Ghosts, Princess and Cat come in)

Princess:	Stop!
Ghosts:	Why are you fighting?
Witch:	I want to control the kingdom.

Prince: She wants to keep me here.

Ghosts: Witch, this is our house and we like them. So right now all of you have to leave.

Witch, Werewolves, Vampires: Fine, we will go.

Witch: But we will return.

Prince: We will see. I will make sure that it never happens.

Witch: Whatever! Let's go.

(The Witch, Vampires and Werewolves exit)

Cat: Princess, can we visit our friends often?

Princess: We can come every day.

Ghosts: It will be so much fun.

Prince: Thank you for helping us. You have proven to be the best friends ever.

THE END

The Vampires & the Princesses

by 1st grade students

Characters:

Blue Princesses

Red Princesses

Narrator

Queen 1

Queen 2

Vampire 1

Vampire 2

Vampire 3

Vampire 4

Vampire 5

Vampire 6

Vampire 7

Vampire 8

Vampire 9

Good Vampire

Ninja

Blue Princesses:	Do you want to go to the store?
Red Princesses:	No.
Blue Princesses:	Do you want to read a book?
Red Princesses:	No.
Blue Princesses:	Do you want to play?
Red Princesses:	No.
Blue Princesses:	Why not?
Red Princesses:	Because we said so.
Blue Princesses:	Well, we are bored.
Narrator:	On the night of Halloween, the Princesses were preparing to go Trick-or-Treating.
Princesses:	Mom, aunt, we want to go Trick or Treating at the house over the hill.

(Queens enter)

Queens:	We don't think it is such a great idea. The people who live there are strange.
Princesses:	Please, we will make sure we are safe.
Queens:	Fine, but you need to go all together and don't get separated.
Princesses:	Yes, we promise.

(Queens and Princesses exit)

Narrator:	Meanwhile inside the house on top of the hill.

Vampire 1:	I am a vampire.
Vampire 2:	You are a vampire.
Vampire 3:	You suck blood.
Vampire 4:	You do too.
Vampire 5:	You are mad.
Vampire 6:	You are mean.
Vampire 7:	We all are.
Vampire 8:	You are evil
Vampire 9:	We all are evil.
Narrator:	So the princesses went to the house over the hill and rang the doorbell.

(Princesses enter)

Vampires:	Hello. Can we help you?
Princesses:	Trick or Treat.
Vampires:	Welcome to our house.
Princesses:	Hey, you are dressed as vampires, cool costume!
Vampires:	Yes, we are. We like these clothes.
Princesses:	Well, can we have some candy.
Vampires:	Sure, let's go to the kitchen to get it.
Narrator:	So the Vampires led the Princesses to the kitchen, but once they were there, the Vampires didn't let them go.

Princesses:	Well, where is our candy?
Vampires:	Candy?
Princesses:	Weren't you going to give us candy. It is Halloween.
Vampires:	Oh no! We don't have candy.
Princesses:	Then I think we need to leave.
Vampires:	You cannot leave. We are going to suck your blood.
Princesses:	Oh no!
Good Vampire:	We cannot do that. They are princesses.
Vampires:	Stay out of this.
Good Vampire:	But we don't need to be mean.
Vampires:	You are a vampire. You can't be nice.
Good Vampire:	Of course I can be nice.
Princesses:	Please help us.
Good Vampire:	I will try to.
Vampires:	Get out of here.
Good Vampire:	Fine, but I will come back.
Vampire 1:	*(to the Princesses)* You stay here.
Vampire 2:	We will lock the door.
Vampire 3:	We are going to see that nobody is around.
Vampire 4:	And then we will return.

Vampire 5:	And suck all your blood.
Princesses:	Oh no!
Vampire 7 and 8:	Oh yes!
Vampire 6:	I love being so evil.

(Vampires exit. Princesses exit)

Narrator:	Meanwhile in the castle.

(Queens enter)

Queen 1:	The girls have taken a long time to return.
Queen 2:	I wonder if they are okay.
Queen 1:	Do you think we should ask for help?
Queen 2:	That is a good idea.
Queen 1:	Who do we call?
Queen 2:	We should call our friend the ninja.
Queen 1:	Great!
Narrator:	The Queens call the ninja.

(Ninja enters)

Ninja:	I am here. How can I help you?
Queen 1:	The Princesses went Trick or Treating.
Queen 2:	But they left a long time ago.
Queen 1:	And they haven't returned.
Ninja:	And you want me to go get them?

Queens:	Yes please.
Ninja:	I will do that.
Queens:	Thank you.
Ninja:	Where did they go?
Queen 1:	To the house at the top of the hill.
Ninja:	The House of the Vampires?
Queen 2:	Vampires?
Ninja:	Yes, that house is full of vampires.
Queens:	Oh no, please save them.
Ninja:	I will, you will have them back in no time.

(Queens and Ninja exit)

Narrator:	Meanwhile at the house.

(Princesses and Good Vampire enter)

Princesses:	Help!
Good Vampire:	I am here to save you.
Princesses:	Good. Because they don't want to let us go.
Good Vampire:	I will take care of this.
Princesses:	Well, Hurry!
Good Vampire:	Don't hurry me up. I am coming.
Princesses:	Just open the door.
Good Vampire:	I am trying. *(He opens the door)*

Princesses:	We are glad you could open the door.
Good Vampire:	You need to hurry before they see us.

(The Vampires enter)

Vampire 1:	Too late.
Vampire 2:	We are here to get you.
Vampire 3:	You are a disgrace for the vampires.
Good Vampire:	I just want to be good.
Vampire 4:	Vampires are not good.
Vampire 5:	We are evil.
Vampire 6:	We also need to suck blood.
Vampire 7:	And the princesses are perfect.
Vampire 8:	We will be full after that.
Vampire 9:	And very happy.
Good Vampire:	I will not be happy.
Vampires:	But we will.
Princesses:	Oh no.

(The Vampires chase the Princesses in slow motion. Ninja enters)

Ninja:	Stop everyone!
Vampire 8:	Who are you?
Ninja:	I am a ninja.
Vampire 2:	So?

Ninja:	I am here to save the princesses.
Vampire 4:	Really?
Vampire 1:	How?
Ninja:	I am fast and I will kick you out of here.
Vampire 5:	But this is our house.
Ninja:	I just want to rescue the princesses.
Vampire 6:	You will have to fight me.
Vampire 7:	If you beat him, the Princesses go with you.
Ninja:	Fine.
Vampire 8:	But if you lose, we suck your blood too.
Princesses:	Please help us.
Ninja:	I will do it.

(Ninja and Vampire 6 fight in slow motion. Ninja wins)

Vampire 2:	Fine, you win.
Vampire 1:	Now get out.
Vampire 8:	And leave us alone.
Vampire 4:	We will find someone else to feed us.
Princesses:	Thank you Ninja, thank you so much.
Good vampire:	Can I go with you?
Princesses:	Sure. You are nice.
Good vampire:	Thank you so much.

(Princesses, Ninja, and Good Vampire exit)

Narrator: So the Princesses, the Ninja and the Good Vampire return to the castle.

(Princesses, Ninja, Good Vampire, and Queens enter)

Queen 1: Princesses, we are so glad to see you!

Queen 2: We were so worried!

Queen 1: What happened?

Princesses: The vampires trapped us.

Queen 2: Vampires?

Princesses: We couldn't escape.

Ninja: I fought with one of them and I won.

Princesses: So we were free to come back here.

Ninja: We brought a friend with us.

Queen 2: Ah!!! A vampire!!!!

Good vampire: Yes, but I am good.

Queen 2: How do we know that?

Princesses: He helped us escape.

Queen 1: You didn't want to harm them?

Good Vampire: No, I wanted to protect them.

Ninja: He really helped.

Queen 2: Fine, he can stay.

Queen 1:	But no sucking blood around here.
Good Vampire:	Oh no! I am a vegetarian.
Queen 2:	A what?
Good Vampire:	I only eat vegetables.
Ninja:	Mmm….I love vegetables.
Queen 2:	Well, let's all go to have a nice salad then.
Princesses:	That sounds delicious.
Queen 1:	This seems to be the end of our adventure.

THE END

The Bad Witch

by 1st. grade students

Characters:

Narrator

Witch

King

Dragons

Princesses

Knight

Explorer

Magic Tiger

Ninjas

Narrator:	A long time ago in a faraway kingdom, there was a witch that wanted the treasure the king had.
Witch:	Give me your treasure.
King:	You cannot have it.
Witch:	Then I am going to call my two dragon friends.
Narrator:	So the witch called her dragon friends.
Witch:	Dragons, dragons come over here.
Dragons:	What do you want?
Witch:	The king didn't want to give me his treasure.
Dragons:	So?
Witch:	I want you to attack the kingdom.
Dragons:	Attack it?
Witch:	Yes, I want you to destroy the castle and kidnap the princesses.
Dragons:	What do we get?
Witch:	You will get part of the treasure when I get it.
Dragons:	Fine.
Narrator:	So the dragons went to the kingdom and took the princesses away.
Dragons:	Princesses, you have to come with us.
Princesses:	We don't want to.
Dragons:	You don't have a choice.
Princesses:	Why not?

Dragons:	Because if you don't come, we will destroy the kingdom.
Narrator:	So the Dragons locked the princesses in the highest tower of the witch's castle. The Dragons stayed right there so they wouldn't escape.
Witch:	Very well dragons.
Princesses:	Get us out of here.
Witch:	No, you cannot leave.
Princesses:	But we don't want to be here.
Witch:	Stop complaining!
Princesses:	We will not.
Witch:	Then I will turn you into a frog.
Narrator:	So the witch transformed all the princesses into frogs. Meanwhile back in the kingdom, the king was very sad so the called the knight, an explorer and four ninjas to rescue the princesses.
King:	Knight, explorer, ninjas, come fast.
All:	Yes, your majesty.
King:	I need you to go rescue the princesses.
All:	Yes, your majesty.
Narrator:	The knight and the explorer knew they would need the help of the magic tiger so they went to the magic forest.
Knight & Explorer:	Tiger, tiger where are you?
Tiger:	I am here.
Knight & Explorer:	We need your help.
Tiger:	What do you want?

Knight & Explorer:	We need to rescue the princesses. The witch turned them into frogs and only your touch can turn them back to normal.
Tiger:	Fine, I will go with you.
Narrator:	So the knight, the explorer, and the tiger started walking towards the witch's castle. Meanwhile the Ninjas were already at the doors of the castle.
Ninja:	Let's knock the doors down.
Ninja:	Yeah, let's fight with them.
Ninja:	Let's rescue the princesses.
Ninja:	And return them to their father.
Ninjas:	Dragons, come out here to fight with us.
Dragons:	Do you think you could beat us?
Ninjas:	We do.
Dragons:	You will have to show us then.
Narrator:	The Dragons and the ninjas started fighting. The ninjas were smart and fast, but the dragons were strong. They fought for three days until the dragons were too tired to fight any more.
Dragons:	We cannot fight any more. We give up.
Ninjas:	We knew we could defeat you.
Dragons:	Just get the princesses out of here.
Ninjas:	We have to wait for the Magic Tiger. Magic Tiger, come over here to save the princesses.
Narrator:	The knight, the explorer and the magic tiger got into the castle to rescue the princesses.

Knight:	Princesses, we are here to save you.
Princesses:	Ribbit!
Explorer:	The magic tiger has to touch you so you can transform into human again.
Princesses:	Ribbit!
Tiger:	I will not eat you, I just need to touch you.
Princesses:	Ribbit!
Narrator:	So the tiger touched the princesses and they became humans again.
Princesses:	Thank you magic tiger.
Tiger:	You are welcome but now we need to go back to the kingdom.
Narrator:	The ninjas found the witch and captured her.
Ninjas:	Witch! You are bad, you have to come with us.
Witch:	Alright! But I will not be happy.
Narrator:	So the ninjas took the witch to the kingdom with them.
Witch:	So what is going to happen to me now?
King:	You have to go to a faraway mountain where you can do no harm.
Ninjas:	What about us?
King:	I will give you gold as a reward.
Knight & Explorer:	And us?
King:	I will give you diamonds.
Princesses:	Father, we want all of them to be our friends.
King:	Sure.
Princesses:	And we want the tiger to stay with us.

King:	If he wants to.
Tiger:	I would love to stay here.
Narrator:	So everyone was happy...except the witch of course.

THE END

In a far away castle

by **2nd. grade students**

Characters:

Narrator 1
Narrator 2
Captain
Boy 1
Girl 1
Girl 2
Boy 2
Sailor
Boy 3
Mad Scientist
Maid
Butler
Zombie 1
Zombie 2
Zombie 3
Zombie 4
Zombie 5
Zombie 6
Zombie 7
Zombie 8
Zombie 9
Magic Fish

Narrator 1:	This story starts in the middle of a storm with a ship rocking back and forth furiously as the waves get higher and higher.
Narrator 2:	Finally, the captain, a sailor, three boys and two girls land safely in an island.
Narrator 1:	But how safe are they really on the island?
Captain:	Oh no, the ship is destroyed, we cannot go back to the ocean.
Boy 1:	Captain, I see a castle right up above the cliff, maybe someone can help us.
Girl 1:	We should try it, it may be our only option.
Girl 2:	That castle looks creepy, I wonder if the rooms inside are pretty.
Boy 2:	Who cares if the rooms are pretty, we need to get some help.
Sailor:	The boy is right captain, we need to go there.
Boy 3:	It looks pretty scary from down here.
Boy 2:	Well, we don't have much of an option, do we?
Girls:	Yes, let's start walking.
Captain:	Fine, let's get going.

===

Narrator 1:	The Captain, the sailor, the boys and the girls started walking towards the castle. However, they didn't know that the castle was owned by a Mad Scientists who was watching from the tower.
Mad Scientist:	I see that they are coming towards the castle.

Maid:	Yes, they are.
Butler:	What would you like us to do?
Mad Scientist:	Prepare the lab, we can trap them and transform them into zombies just like the rest of the sailors.
Maid:	Should we call the zombies so they prepare to attack?
Mad Scientist:	Yes, call them immediately.
Narrator 2:	While the butler and the maid called the zombies, our heroes walked steadily towards the castle.
Boy 3:	You know? I have heard the legend of the Magic Fish.
Boy 2:	The Magic Fish?
Boy 3:	Yes, they say that in a remote island there was a bunch of zombies that can be transformed into people again by a magic fish.
Girl 1:	Maybe this is the island.
Sailor:	No, that just happens on TV.
Captain:	I wouldn't be too sure, strangest things have happened.
Girl 2:	Well, if that is true, then we would need to save the zombies.
Boy 1:	Of course we would, but I am sure there is nothing going on.

==

Narrator 1:	Meanwhile in the castle.
Mad Scientist:	Well, did you find them?
Butler:	Here they are Ms.
Mad Scientist:	Zombies, listen. There is a group of people coming towards the castle, I need some of you to go attack

	them and some of you to make sure the Magic Fish doesn't escape.
Zombies:	Yeah, yeah.
Maid:	The Magic Fish is locked in the tower where it has a golden pond.
Zombies:	Yeah, yeah.
Mad Scientist:	What are you waiting for? Go, go
Zombies:	Yeah, yeah. (*zombies exit*)
Mad Scientist:	Now. Let's plan what we should do with our guests.
Butler:	What about serving them fried brains?
Mad Scientist:	That sounds good.
Maid:	What about a good drink made out of blood?
Mad Scientist:	Even better.
Butler:	I am starting to get hungry.
Mad Scientist:	Concentrate, the food and drinks are not for you...they are for our guests (evil laugh).
Maid:	Well, we can always have a little of that, right?
Mad Scientist:	Maybe...if they don't eat everything. Let's go check where they are from the tower.

==

Narrator 2:	The Zombies go to the forest where they can scare people and the other ones go to the tower.
Narrator 1:	The Zombies in the tower talked to the Magic Fish.
Zombie 1:	Magic Fish you cannot escape.
Magic Fish:	Don't be silly, if you let me go I could help you get back to normal.

Zombie 2:	What if that doesn't happen?
Magic Fish:	It will happen, but for it to happen three boys and two girls would have to understand what real friendship is.
Zombie 3:	We cannot let you go right now. They will have to come get you.
Zombie 1:	Our orders are strict, we have to watch you so you don't escape.
Magic Fish:	Oh brother! So what then?
Zombie 1:	You just keep on swimming.
Magic Fish:	You know that if a girl or a boy guesses my name I can transform you back into sailors?
Zombie 2:	We are zombies now, we don't care about being sailors again.
Zombie 3:	Speak for yourself, I want to be a sailor again...I liked going in the sea.
Magic Fish:	So maybe you can let me go so I can go find a boy or a girl to help me.
Zombie 3:	No, we cannot let that happen. If we let you go the Mad Scientist will be even more furious.
Magic Fish:	Fine, suit yourself, don't complain later then.
Narrator 2:	Meanwhile in the jungle.
Zombie 4:	I think we can surround them and attack them.
Zombie 5:	What if they run towards the beach again?
Zombie 6:	That is why three of us go behind them and three of us go in front.
Zombie 7:	That sounds good.

Zombie 8:	What should we do with them afterwards?
Zombie 9:	Weren't you paying attention? Ms. Mad told us to get them to her.
Zombie 4:	I wonder what she is planning to do.
Zombie 5:	I guess she will transform them into zombies like us.
Zombie 6:	Yes! More of us to suck the blood and crush bones.
Zombie 7:	We are more than enough already.
Zombie 8:	No, we can always be more.
Zombie 9:	So are we going to just talk or should we go?
Zombie 4:	Zombie cheer first!

(zombies do zombie cheer)

Captain:	Oh no, this is terrible, the boat is destroyed and look at those zombies coming from the castle.
Boy 2:	Oh the zombies will never get us. We can get back to the ship and fight from there.
Sailor:	Get back to the ship, really? How would that help if it is destroyed already.
Girl 1:	Well, our only option is to go on and get to the castle.
Sailor:	Let's move on, I have heard that zombies like brains.
Boy 1:	What if we just hide behind the trees and then when they go towards the boat we run the other way towards the castle.
Girl 2:	That is not a bad idea.
Boy 3:	Come on, let's move fast, they are coming.

(Zombies 4, 5, 6, 7 appear)

Zombies:	Brains, brains, we want brains. Lungs, lungs, we eat lungs!
Zombie 4:	Wait, I smell something.
Zombie 5:	It is nothing, you have been craving brains for too long.
Zombie 6:	Let's go to get them.
Zombie 7:	To the ship!
Zombies:	Brains, brains, we want brains. Lungs, lungs, we eat lungs!

(Zombies exit)

Captain:	Uff! That was a close one.
Sailor:	Yes. Let's head to the castle.

(They exit)

Narrator 1:	Meanwhile in the castle.

(Butler with Zombies 8, 9, 10)

Butler:	The Mad Scientist wants you to protect the castle.
Zombie 8:	Really? What do we get for that?
Butler:	you get to keep your life.
Zombie 9:	We are already death.
Butler:	Oh yeah.
Zombie 8:	So, what then?
Butler:	You can eat the brains of the people that come to the castle.
Zombie 10:	Brains are delicious. Deal.

(Maid appears)

Maid:	What are you doing here?
Zombie 10:	Just receiving instructions.

Maid:	Well, while you are getting your instructions, a group of people has already arrived to the door of the castle.
Zombie 8:	Fine, we will be there.
Narrator 2:	So the zombies went towards the door of the castle where but the Mad Scientist was already there.

(Captain knocks at the door)

Mad Scientist:	*(talking to the Zombies)* Where were you? This wasn't supposed to happen.
Zombie 9:	We were talking to the butler.
Mad Scientist:	Now I have to receive those people and my chances of catching them are slim.
Zombie 10:	We will catch them for you.
Mad Scientist:	The other zombies were supposed to catch them but they missed them in the jungle.
Captain:	Is there anyone here?
Mad Scientist:	Just a moment.

(Maid coming in)

Maid:	Coming, coming.

(Maid opens the door. The Captain, the Sailor, the boys and girls come in)

Captain:	We are lost, our ship broke and we need help.
Mad Scientist:	Help? What kind of help?
Sailor:	We need a place to stay overnight.
Mad Scientist:	We can arrange that *(evil laugh)*.
Girl 1:	*(whispering to Girl 2)* That was creepy.
Girl 2:	Super creepy.
Boy 1:	And we need some food.

Maid:	We have some delicious brains…I mean broccoli.
Boy 2:	Uggh! I don't like broccoli.
Boy 3:	Be quiet!
Captain:	Thank you so much, we won't be any trouble.
Narrator 1:	Meanwhile in the ship.
Zombie 4:	There is no one here.
Zombie 5:	I told you I smelled something back in the jungle.
Zombie 6:	Now we have to go back.
Zombie 7:	And I am sooooo hungry.
Zombie 4:	Stop complaining, start walking.
Narrator 2:	A few hours went by and night came along…it was a night that everyone would remember.
Girl 1:	This castle really has nice rooms, we should go explore.
Boy 1:	But it is too dark, it is kind of creepy.
Girl 2:	You are not scared, are you?
Boy 1:	Me? Of course not!
Boy 2:	It would be super cool to go look around.
Boy 3:	What are we waiting for? Let's go.
Girl 1:	Should we let the captain know?
Boy 2:	Nah, both the captain and the sailor are already snoring.
Narrator 2:	So the boys and the girls went to explore the castle. They walked up and down discovering many rooms until they got to the tower.
Girl 1:	Look, there is a door with a rainbow on it.
Girl 2:	Maybe the Magic Fish is inside.
Boy 1:	So let's go in.

Narrator 2:	The boys and girls open the door.
Boy 2:	Look over there, there is a huge fish tank.
Magic Fish:	I am over here.

(boys and girls approach the tank)

Magic Fish:	Be careful. There are three zombies around here.
Boy 3:	We are not scared of z...

(Zombie 1, 2, and 3 appear)

Zombie 1:	What are you doing here?
Zombie 2:	We have orders to protect the Magic Fish.
Zombie 3:	And we want to eat your brains.
Zombies:	Brains, brains, we love brains.
Boy 2:	Stop! We don't want you to eat us.
Magic Fish:	If you guess my name I can help you.
Boy 1:	Your name?
Zombie 1:	You won't be able to guess it.
Zombie 2:	We all tried before being zombies.
Zombie 3:	And we failed so the Mad Scientist transformed us into zombies.
Girl 2:	So if we don't guess it we get transformed into zombies?
Zombie 1:	Yes.
Boy 3:	We will get it, don't worry.
Magic Fish:	Think about what is more important to you.
Boy 1:	My family is important.
Magic Fish:	Other than your family.
Boy 2:	Being healthy is important.

Magic Fish:	No, no, more than that. Let me give you a clue. What are you?
Girl 1:	Girls?
Boy 3:	Boys?
Girl 2:	Students?
Magic Fish:	Yes, but between all of you.
Boy 2:	I got it! We are friends!
Boy 1:	Is Friendship your name?
Magic Fish:	Yes, that is my name. Now I can turn the zombies into sailors again.

(Magic Fish touches the zombies, they transform into sailors)

Zombie 1:	I am back to normal.
Zombie 2:	This feels fantastic.
Zombie 3:	I can't wait to leave the island.

(Captain and Sailor come in)

Captain:	What is going on?
Sailor:	Who are you guys? Where did you come from?
Zombie 1:	The magic fish transformed us again into people.
Zombie 2:	Now we can help you rebuild your ship and we can all leave.
Zombie 3:	We need to hurry up.

(The Mad Scientist, the Maid, the Butler and the rest of the Zombies come in)

Mad Scientist:	What? How could this happen?
Girl 1:	Well, we guessed the name of the Magic Fish.
Mad Scientist:	Zombies, attack them!

Zombie 4:	Actually, we would like the Magic Fish to touch us so we can be sailors again.
Mad Scientist:	Fine, Maid, Butler - attack them!
Maid & Butler:	No, we are tired of you ordering us around. We will leave in the ship.
Mad Scientist:	You are betraying me.
Maid & Butler:	Yes, we are. You have no power over us anymore.
Zombies:	Neither over us. We are free!
Magic Fish:	I think I can make a rainbow shine to celebrate.
Girl 1:	I love rainbows!
Narrator 1:	And this is the end of the story. All the sailors rebuilt the ship and everyone left the island, except the Magic Fish and the Mad Scientist.
Mad Scientist:	Magic Fish grant me my wish!
Magic Fish:	No, you have to guess my name first.
Mad Scientist:	Nooooooo!
Narrator 2:	And to this day, you can still hear the Mad Scientist saying name after name...but he would never say the magic word: Friendship. The End.

THE END

The Stolen Chicken

by 3rd. grade students

Characters:

Narrator

Dance Teacher

Melissa

Mary

Amelia

Thief 1

Thief 2

Oscar

Justin

Junior

Police 1

Police 2

Narrator:	It is the middle of January, the girls have been working really hard on their dance routine to compete in the National Dance Competition to be held in February. This is their last week of practice.
Dance teacher:	Hurry up and get ready. We have to work really hard this week because the dance festival is next week. Hey Melissa, I still haven't got that slip for the trip to that school.
Melissa:	Oh, that's what I wanted to talk to you about. Can I give it to you tomorrow?
Dance teacher:	I believe you can't. Do you have it right now?
Melissa:	Yes, but it is not signed, I forgot to give it to my mom.
Dance teacher:	Well, I am sorry but this has to be done today. I am not sure what to do.
Mary:	Melissa, maybe we can go to mom's work so she can sign it and then come back.
Melissa:	Do you think we have enough time?
Amelia:	I can go with you. I know a short cut through the forest that can save us some time.
Dance teacher:	I am not too sure about this.
Melissa:	Please teacher, otherwise I won't be able to go with you to the trip.
Mary:	We will go together, nothing will happen.
Dance teacher:	Very well then. I will call your mom so she knows you are on your way.

Amelia:	I will let my brother know too. After all he is older so if by any chance we have a problem he can help us out.
Dance teacher:	Fine, I will see you later then.
Narrator:	The girls head out the dance studio and walk towards the restaurant where Melissa and Mary's mom works.
Amelia:	Just follow me. This is a road that almost no one follows because it cuts through the woods. I have been here a lot and it is very safe.
Mary:	I hope you are right because this is a little scary to me.
Melissa:	Nothing will happen, don't worry. We have to hurry up.
Mary:	What is that?
Amelia:	That noise? It is probably a squirrel, there are many in this part of the woods.
Mary:	No, not that...it sounds like a chicken.
Melissa:	A chicken? Stop watching TV, you are imagining things.
Mary:	No, really. Just listen.

(Chicken noises are heard)

Amelia:	Someone's coming. Hide.
Thief 1:	You need to put that chicken away.
Thief 2:	Away where?
Thief 1:	I am not sure, hide it under your jacket or something.
Thief 2:	It wasn't my idea to steal a chicken.
Thief 1:	Well, that wasn't the plan. The plan is to go for the car but when the farmer found out we were trying to rob him, the only thing I could think about was to steal a chicken.

Thief 2:	Now what?
Thief 1:	I know for a fact that this chicken won a prize in the last County Fair so I know that the farmer will want to keep it alive.
Thief 2:	Not following you.
Thief 1:	We keep the chicken and we ask for money. Until he gives us money we don't return the chicken.
Thief 2:	Oh, I see...that is clever.
Thief 1:	Of course it is. All my ideas are clever!
Thief 2:	Whatever.
(They exit)	
Melissa:	Oh no, this is not good.
Amelia:	We should follow them and rescue the chicken.
Mary:	I don't think so, we need to go back to dance class.
Melissa:	Yes but this is important.
Mary:	Dance class is important too.
Melissa:	I think that you are the chicken! *(laughs)*
Mary:	I am not!
Melissa:	You are!
Amelia:	Girls, stop fighting. Come on, let's go after them.
Narrator:	The girls follow the thieves to their hide out. They were hiding in a shack in the middle of the forest.
Melissa:	Come here, I think we can look through the window.
Amelia:	Be quiet, I don't want them to hear us.
Mary:	I am trying. *(she trips and falls down)* Ouch!
Melissa:	Mary, are you okay?

Thief 1:	Who is there?
Amelia:	Oh no, they heard us.
Thief 2:	Let's go look.
Mary:	I am sorry.
Melissa:	It is not your fault.

(The thieves come out)

Melissa:	Hi, we are kind of lost and we were wondering if you could tell us which way to go.
Thief 1:	Where do you want to go?
Amelia:	Well, we are heading downtown.

(Thief 2 tries to hide the chicken behind his back)

Mary:	Hey what are you doing?
Thief 2:	Nothing.
Mary:	What do you have in your hand?
Thief 2:	Nothing.
Mary:	Is that a chicken?
Melissa:	Mary, be quiet!
Thief 2:	What if it is?
Mary:	Is it yours?
Thief 2:	Now it is.
Amelia:	Well, we need to go. *(tries to pull Mary away)*
Mary:	What do you mean by "Now it is"? It wasn't before?
Thief 1:	Look girl, you are asking too many questions.
Mary:	Did you steal it?
Thief 1:	I told you that you are asking too many questions.
Mary:	Oh my God! You stole this chicken.

Thief 1:	Well, yes I did but now you will need to come with me because I can't allow you tell anyone.
Mary:	What?
Thief 1:	You are coming with me.
Mary:	Noooo.
Amelia:	Take your hands off her!
Thief 1:	Matt, bring the rope. I think we need to tie them up, that way they don't escape.
Melissa:	What? No, we need to get to Dance class.
Thief 1:	Well, I guess you are going to be a little late.
Thief 2:	*(brings the rope)* Here it is.

(The thieves tie the girls up)

Thief 1:	Now girls, you need to be quiet until we get the money from the farmer.
Thief 2:	Yeah, we can't let you go until then.
Mary:	What if we scream?
Thief 1:	Well, then we would have to call your parents and ask them for money too.
Melissa:	And if we are quiet?
Thief 1:	Then we will let you go after we get the money for the chicken and no harm done.
Amelia:	Fine, we will be quiet.
Thief 2:	Good.
Narrator:	Meanwhile, at the dance studio, the teacher was starting to get concerned.

Dance Teacher: *(on the phone)* Hi, Mrs. Smith. This is the Dance Teacher. Did the girls get there already? No? They left a long time ago. Let me call Amelia's brother to see if he picked them up. Yes, I will let you know. / Hello?

Oscar: Yes.

Dance Teacher: This is the dance teacher. I was wondering if you have seen Amelia and her friends?

Oscar: No, why?

Dance Teacher: Well, they left my class a long time ago and they were going to come back but they haven't.

Oscar: Yeah, Amelia called me when she left your class but I haven't heard back from her.

Dance Teacher: Well, I will wait for a little more but will call the police if they don't come back soon.

Oscar: Sounds good. I will call my friends and go look for them.

Dance Teacher: Great. Thank you.

Narrator: So Oscar gathered his friends and started looking for the girls.

Oscar: I know that Amelia usually walks through the forest to save time.

Justin: Then I guess we need to go there.

Junior: Let's try to get there before it gets dark.

Oscar: So, come on, what are we waiting for?!

Narrator: Meanwhile in the forest.

Amelia: Oh no, it is getting dark and we are stuck here without a chance of getting away.

Melissa:	I don't even want to try to escape because if they call my mom, she will be really upset with us.
Mary:	So? We just have to wait then?
Amelia:	It seems like it.
Thief 1:	Okay girls. The farmer is going to leave the money for us later today. Until that happens you have to stay here.
Melissa:	But then it will be too late for us to go back to dance class.
Thief 2:	Yes but at least you will be on time to get back home.
Thief 1:	Where did you leave the chicken?
Thief 2:	I thought you had it.
Thief 1:	What? No, you had it all the time.
Thief 2:	Oh no, we should look for it.
Thief 1:	Don't try anything funny, girls...

(The thieves leave while looking for the chicken)

Narrator:	The police were already looking for the thieves when they found the boys in the forest.
Police 1:	Boys, by any chance have you seen a chicken around here?
Justin:	No.
Police 2:	What are you doing all by yourselves?
Junior:	Just going to...
Oscar:	We were going to pick up my sister from her dance class.

Police 1:	Well, hurry up. It is about to get dark and the forest is not very safe after dark.
Justin:	We will, officer.
Police 2:	Call us if you see anything.
Oscar:	Will do.

(Police exit)

Oscar:	Well, that was strange.
Junior:	Look Oscar, there is a chicken running at us.
Justin:	It looks scared. Maybe that is the chicken the police were talking about.
Oscar:	Here chicken, chicken. *(Oscar grabs the chicken)*
Junior:	I wonder how it got here.
Justin:	Yeah, the forest is no place for chickens.

(The thieves come running after the chicken)

Thief 1:	Hey boys...that is my chicken.
Oscar:	Oh, really?
Thief 2:	Yes, it escaped from its coop.
Oscar:	Okay then, I guess you can have it back.
Thief 1:	Thank you so much. Well, have a great evening.
Justin:	You too.

(The thieves leave)

Justin:	You know? Those two guys look very suspicious.
Oscar:	Yes, they seemed to be too nervous.
Junior:	Do you think they are hiding something?
Oscar:	Probably. We should follow them.
Justin:	Yeah, let's follow them. Maybe they saw your sister.

Junior:	Should we call the police?
Oscar:	No. What for? We don't really know anything.
Narrator:	So the boys started following the thieves until they get to the shed where the girls are held captive.
Oscar:	Oh my! Amelia, what happened?
Amelia:	Oscar, I am so glad you are here.
Junior:	What happened?
Melissa:	Well, we were going to get a signature from my mom when we saw two thieves with a chicken so we decided to follow them...
Mary:	And they caught us!
Justin:	Well, I am glad you are safe. Let's get out of here.
Thief 1:	Not so fast.
Thief 2:	You cannot leave.
Oscar:	Look, we don't want to fight. Whatever you stole, you will have to return.
Thief 1:	We don't want to go to jail so you cannot leave until we receive the money.
Justin:	What will you do if we try to leave?
Thief 2:	We can call your parents and tell them you are about to die.
Junior:	Well, that is not true.
Thief 2:	No, it is not but they don't know that.

(From behind the thieves appear two policemen/women)

Police 1:	Don't move
Police 2:	Put your hands in the air.

Police 1:	We have been looking for you all day.
Thief 1:	How did you find us?
Police 1:	We followed the boys. It was pure luck that we found them.

(Dance Teacher appears)

Dance Teacher:	Oh girls, are you okay?
Amelia:	We are fine.
Mary:	I got a little scared.
Oscar:	We found them just in time.
Police 1:	What happened girl?
Mary:	We were following the thieves to try to save the chicken, but they caught us.
Police 2:	Well, I am glad you are safe.
Amelia:	*(to the Dance Teacher)* How did you find us?
Dance Teacher:	Your brother told me that he was going to come look for you if you didn't appear on time. I just followed the route you would take to get downtown.
Melissa:	Well, I am sorry but I still don't have the signed form.
Dance Teacher:	Let's get you home and your mom can sign it there.
Police 1:	*(to the thieves)* And you...you are going to spend a long time in jail.
Thief 1:	For a chicken?
Police 2:	Not only for that but also for attempted kidnapping.
Thief 2:	*(to Thief 1)* I told you stealing a chicken was a bad idea.
Thief 1:	Just be quiet.

Narrator: So the girls won the dance competition, the boys got a medal of honor for their courage, and the thieves went to jail for a very, very long time. The End.

THE END

The Magic Fish

by 3rd. grade students

Characters:

Narrator 1

Ashley

Whiskers, the Cat

Mom

Dad

Jose (brother)

Emily

Annie

Kanera

Cindy

Asbelle (custodian)

Isabelle (custodian)

Narrator 2

Narrator 3

Magic Fish

Ghost 1

Ghost 2

Ghost 3

Spikes, the dog

Narrator 1:   Our story starts at Ashley's house on a Friday in October.

(Ashley crying. Whiskers, the cat comes in)

Whiskers: Ashley, why are you crying?

Ashley: Spikes is gone, I cannot find him anywhere.

(Mom comes in)

Mom: *(to Whiskers)* I thought I told you to get out of the kitchen!

Whiskers: Meow!

(Dad comes in)

Dad: Shikira, don't talk to the cat like that...after all, he cannot answer.

Whiskers: If only they knew I can.

(Jose comes in)

Jose: Dad, I can take the cat out of the kitchen.

Dad: Very well, also take the dog with you.

(Ashley cries more)

Mom: What is wrong sweetie?

Ashley: Spikes is not here, I don't know where he is.

Whiskers: Maybe we finally got rid of him.

Ashley: Whiskers, don't say that.

Jose: Say what? He just meowed.

Dad: Oh Ashley, I am sure he will come back.

Jose: Ashley, I think you should go find him.

Mom: That could be dangerous.

Ashley: I can go with my friends.

Jose:	I think I saw Spikes running towards the amusement park.
Dad:	You can go look for him only if your friends go with you.
Mom:	And you have to return before dinner.
Whiskers:	And hopefully you won't find him.
Ashley:	Whiskers, don't say that!
Jose:	Ashley, I think you are going crazy, the cat just meowed.
Ashley:	Whatever Jose, you just don't understand him.
Dad:	Ok, go and be careful.
Narrator 1:	So Ashley called her friends so they could go together to the abandoned amusement park to find Spikes.
Emily:	When did he disappear?
Ashley:	Today in the morning.
Annie:	We need to go together to find it.
Kanera:	Let's go to the amusement park to find your dog. You will be really sad if we don't find it.
Emily:	We should call my sister Cindy to come with us. After all, she is already fourteen.
Ashley:	Good idea.
Narrator 1:	So the girls, called Cindy.
Cindy:	*(on the phone)* Okay, I will go with you but only because I have heard that the amusement park is scary and I love scary places.
Narrator 1:	So the five girls get to the amusement park.
Girls:	Spikes, spikes where are you?

(The Custodians – Isabelle and Asbelle - appear)

Asbelle:	What are you doing here?

Cindy:	We are looking for her dog, he got lost in the morning and her brother saw him coming this way.
Isabelle:	Well, the amusement park is closed. It is rusty and we are cleaning.
Emily:	Why are you cleaning it now?
Asbelle:	I couldn't get my work done because the ghosts were knocking at my door a lot yesterday night.
Kanera:	Ghosts?
Isabelle:	Yes, there are a lot of ghosts in this park. Ever since the cart on the roller coaster broke down and a lot of people died in one single day.
Annie:	That is terrible.
Asbelle:	There is only one thing that can change those ghosts into people again.
Cindy:	Really? What?
Isabelle:	A gentle touch from the magic fish.
Ashley:	A magic fish?
Narrator 1:	The custodians explained to the girls the legend of the magic fish.
Narrator 2:	A long time ago in the middle of the amusement park there was a pond that everyone used as a wishing well.
Narrator 3:	When the roller coaster broke, a magician came and transformed the gold fish that lived in there into a magic fish that could turn the people back to normal.

Narrator 2:	However, he named the fish a special name and only the person that can guess its name will be able to use its powers to transform the people back again.
Narrator 3:	Up to now a lot of people have tried but no one had been able to guess.
Annie:	I am sure we will be able to guess.
Isabelle:	Well, if you do that we will help you find your dog.
Asbelle:	I saw him coming in but then he hid and I haven't seen him since the morning.
Cindy:	Show us where the pond is.
Narrator 1:	So Isabelle and Asbelle showed the girls the magic pond where the fish was happily swimming.
Girls:	Magic fish, magic fish, would you help us transform these people?
Magic Fish:	Yes, I would. But first you have to guess my name, you have three guesses.
Emily:	Will you give us a clue?
Magic Fish:	Think about the person you love the most.
Kanera:	I love my brother.
Emily:	I love my sister.
Cindy:	I love my grandma.
Annie:	I love my dad.
Ashley:	I love my mom.
Cindy:	Those are a lot of names to guess from.
Magic Fish:	Think about what those people are for you. That is my name, the people you love the most.

Kanera: Well, my brother is my friend.

Emily: My sister is my companion.

Cindy: My grandma is my teacher.

Annie: My dad is my support.

Ashley: I think I know what the Magic Fish is asking...all of those people are our Family. Do you think that is her name?

Emily: We should try.

Ashley: Is your name Family?

Magic Fish: Very well!!! Yes, that is my name...the most important people in the world.

Narrator 1: So the girls guided the Magic Fish to the entrance of the roller coaster, where ghosts started appearing.

Ghost 1: Booo...go away, don't get in the roller coaster or all of you will die.

Ghost 2: You have been warned. Booo!!! Go away or you will die in here.

Magic Fish: I am scared, I shouldn't have come here.

Ghost 3: This is your last warning, if you don't leave, we will put you on the roller coaster and you will all die.

Magic Fish: Wait, I know the ghosts are saying that to scare us and protect us. They probably just want to be human again.

Ashley: Well, it IS a little scary for me.

Cindy: Nothing to fear. Magic Fish, will you touch them on the hand so they live again.

Magic Fish: Of course.

Narrator 1:	The magic fish touched each one of the ghosts in the hand and they became people again.
Ghost 1:	Thank you Magic Fish. It has been so long since I was human.
Ghost 2:	Thank you girls. We owe you.
Ashley:	You are welcome but...have you seen my dog?
Ghost 3:	Yes, I know exactly where he is...let me bring him to you. He was just scared.
Narrator 1:	The ghost now turned into human went to get the dog Spikes.
Spikes:	Ashley, I missed you so much. I was scared.
Ashley:	Spikes, I missed you too. I am so happy to see you.
Annie:	Well, now that you have found him, let's go home...it is getting dark.

(Isabelle and Asbelle come in)

Isabelle:	*(to the ghosts)* Would you help us clean the amusement park so we can open it again?
Ghost 1:	Yes, that is a great idea.
Magic Fish:	I will send a rainbow over it so it is full of color.
Asbelle:	Thank you girls. Feel free to come any time you want once the park reopens.
Narrator 1:	And Ashley arrived back home with Spikes.
Dad:	Ashley! I am glad you are back, and I see you brought Spikes with you.
Whiskers:	Oh great! He is back again.
Spikes:	Listen you! Don't mess up with me or I will bite you.

Ashley: Yes dad, everything is back to normal.

THE END

Mirrorland

by 4th. Grade Students

Characters:

Narrator 1

Narrator 2

Amy

Lisa

Mary

Keisha

John

Soldier 1

Soldier 2

Haunted Nurse

Rick

Al

Guard 1

Guard 2

Guard 3

Guard 4

Witch

Queen

Narrator 1:	Our story takes place on a snowy afternoon in the middle of January.
Narrator 2:	It was not snowy, and it was November.
Narrator 1:	It was snowy!
Narrator 2:	Okay then, but it was November.
Narrator 1:	Fine. Our story takes place on a snowy afternoon in the middle of November.
Narrator 2:	*(whispering)* It wasn't snowing.
Amy:	Are you done you two?
Narrator 1:	Sure, go ahead.
Amy:	Thank you so much.

(Lisa, Mary, and Keisha come in)

Lisa:	*(coming in)* The cookies are almost done, five more minutes or so.
Mary:	What movie are we going to watch?
Keisha:	Didn't we say we would watch The Hunger Games?
Lisa:	I thought we would watch Batman.
Keisha:	Only if the boys came but so far they haven't decided.
Amy:	Well, if they don't come, we could play with make-up and do our nails.
Mary:	And if they come, we can put make-up on them and do THEIR nails. *(They all laugh)*
Keisha:	Sure, I would love to see Rick all made-up.
Lisa:	*(imitating a boy)* Oh look at my nails... *(they laugh)*

(The telephone rings)

Amy:	Hello?

(All the girls try to listen to the conversation)

John: Hey, are we still on for the movie?

Amy: That is exactly what we were talking about.

John: We will be there in 30 minutes, we just need a ride from my mom.

Amy: The girls and I were wondering if you wanted a make-over. *(laughs)*

John: What?

Amy: You know, your nails and make-up done. *(laughs)*

John: You are crazy.

Amy: Whatever.

John: We will be there soon.

Amy: *(hanging up the phone)* They will be here in 30 minutes and no, they don't want a make-over.

Keisha: Well, while we wait, let's try this make-up on.

Mary: I found this mirror at my house and I brought it today.

Lisa: Wow! That mirror looks fancy.

Mary: My mom mentioned a long time ago that this mirror has magic powers.

Keisha: Sure, whatever.

Mary: No, really, she says that it can transport you to another place.

Amy: If that is true, I am not sure we should play with the mirror.

Keisha: I am sure it is perfectly fine, nothing will happen.

Lisa: Well, just in case, put it down.

Mary:	Okay.
Keisha:	Hey, what happened to the cookies?
Lisa:	Oh my, I forgot, let me go get them.
Amy:	I will go with you, finding the plates in my kitchen can be tricky.

(Amy and Lisa exit)

Keisha:	*(Showing Mary a little bag of make-up)* Look what I have here. *(She takes out a lipstick)*
Mary:	Keisha, that color is not good for you, it is too red.
Keisha:	Of course it is good for me. Give me the mirror.
Mary:	Lisa said we should put it down.
Keisha:	What do they know? Give it.
Mary:	No, we shouldn't play with the mirror.
Keisha:	I said I would take it.

(Mary and Keisha fight over the mirror. The mirror transports them to another place)

Mary:	Where are we?
Keisha:	I am not sure.
Soldier 1:	Who are you?
Soldier 2:	*(whispering to Soldier 1)* They look very suspicious.
Mary:	My name is Mary.
Keisha:	And I am Keisha.
Soldier 2:	Ahhhh! They are witches!
Soldier 1:	Get a hold of yourself. What is wrong with you?
Mary:	We certainly are NOT witches.
Soldier 2:	You appeared out of nowhere just like the other witch.

Soldier 1:   And the crazy nurse.

Keisha: Crazy nurse?

Soldier 1:   Silence! You have no right to talk. If you don't obey us,
all of us will arrest you.

Keisha: All of you?

Soldier 1:   Yeah.

Mary: What are you talking about? You two are the only
soldiers here.

Soldiers: Oh yeah.

Soldier 2:   Well, then...go make a sculpture of us.

Mary: What?

Soldier 2:   It seemed like something good to say.

Keisha: Oh geez! Where are we?

Soldier 1:   In Mirrorland.

Keisha & Mary: Mirror what?

Soldier 2:   land.

Mary: I know Keisha, I think this is a joke. Very funny Amy and
Lisa, now get us back to your house.

Keisha: Mary, I don't think this is a joke.

Soldier 1:   If you are not witches then you should come with us.

Mary: Really, why?

Soldier 2:   Because it is almost midnight and at midnight the
Haunted Nurse comes out of the castle looking for blood.

Keisha: Say what?

Soldier 1:   A long time ago, a nurse crossed the portal. We didn't get
to her on time so the witch found her. She turned her

into a zombie with big nails, sharp teeth, and crazy hair. Since then, every night at midnight she comes out of the castle looking for blood. The only thing that can turn her into human again are chocolate chip cookies, but in this kingdom we don't have them.

Haunted Nurse: Blood, brains, cookies! Blood, brains, cookies!

Soldier 2: Hurry up, she is coming. Let's go!

Narrator 1: Meanwhile, Amy and Lisa return with the cookies to the room where Keisha and Mary were.

Amy: Here they...hey, where are they?

Lisa: I am not sure, maybe they went to the bathroom.

(Doorbell rings, Amy opens the door)

John: Hey, we are here. Let the movie start!

Amy: Well, we have to wait. Keisha and Mary were here but we are not sure where they are.

Rick: Oh come on! Where can they be? Your house only has two bedrooms and one bathroom.

Amy: I know, but they aren't there.

Al: Aha! This sounds like a mystery.

Lisa: Be quiet! We are worried and you are turning this into a joke.

Al: What?

John: Look, nothing could have happened to them if they were just here a few minutes ago.

Rick: You know, if we are not going to watch a movie, I'd rather go to McDonalds to get a cheese burger and large fries.

Amy:	Is that the only thing you think about?
Rick:	Pretty much.
Lisa:	Well, here, have some cookies meanwhile.
Rick:	Fine, I will take one and keep a few in my pocket just in case I get hungry.
John:	So, when was the last time you saw them?
Amy:	We were waiting for you guys and Lisa and I went to get the cookies from the kitchen.
John:	What were you doing before heading to the kitchen?
Amy:	Not sure.
Lisa:	Oh yeah, we were talking about a mirror.
Al:	A mirror?
Lisa:	Yes. We were going to play with make-up and do our nails while we waited for you guys. Mary brought a strange looking mirror from home and we were talking about it.
Al:	Did Mary mention anything about the mirror?
Amy:	Yes, she said the mirror was magic.
Al:	I knew it!
All:	What?
Al:	My dad told me that a long time ago there was a legend regarding a magic mirror that could transport people to another dimension.
John:	Get out of here!
Al:	No, really. Apparently a nurse disappeared through the mirror and they never heard from her again.

Rick:	Do you think Keisha and Mary traveled through the mirror?
Al:	I'm almost sure that is what happened.
Amy:	So how do we get them back?
Al:	We need to find an underground portal. If I am not mistaken, there are several portals through the ice-cream trucks.
Rick:	Mmmm, ice cream.
Al:	Come on, this is serious.
Rick:	Okay, I get it. But there is nothing wrong with looking for the portal and getting ice cream at the same time.
Narrator 2:	So the children went to look for an ice cream truck. Each one of them got their favorite flavor and as soon as they tasted it, they were transported to Mirrorland.
Amy:	Well, we are here, now what?
John:	I guess we have to look for them.
Lisa:	And how do you suppose we do that?
Al:	We should look for a construction of some sort...a castle maybe.
Rick:	Stop talking, someone's coming.
John:	What should we do now?
Amy:	Well, one of you has to talk to them to find out where we are at.
Al:	I'll do it, just listen to see if we can get some information.

(Three guards come marching in)

Guard 1:	What are you doing in the property and who are you?
Al:	I am a guard like you.
Guard 2:	What's your name?
Al:	No name.
Guard 1:	Okay No name, you are a fake guard.
Al:	No, believe me, I am a guard like you.
Guard 2:	In your dreams.
Al:	Hey, how did you know I dream about being like you.
Guard 2:	It was a guess.
Guard 3:	Are you saying we watch you when you sleep?
Al:	I didn't say that, you did.
Guard 3:	Geez, no sense of humor.
Guard 1:	Okay, you can go into the enchanted forest.
Al:	Why would I want to do that?
Guard 1:	That is where everyone is going since those witches appeared out of nowhere.
Al:	Witches?
Guard 2:	Yes, two witches that looked like girls appeared in the middle of the forest, the Haunted Nurse tried catching them but she couldn't. Since then the Witch has been furious. We all gathered inside the enchanted forest to protect ourselves.
Al:	So those two new witches are there too?
Guard 3:	Yes.
Al:	Great! Go ahead, I will follow you shortly.
Guard 1:	Very well then, just be aware of the Haunted Nurse.

(Guards leave)

Rick: Well, now we know where they are. Now what?

John: We should separate. Two of us should go get Keisha and Mary, one of us should go spy on the witch to make sure she is not following us back to Amy's house, and the other two should look for the Haunted Nurse, maybe we can help her.

Rick: I will go look for the Haunted Nurse. Al, are you coming with me?

Al: Sure.

Lisa: Amy and I will go get Keisha and Mary.

John: Fine, I guess I will go spy on the witch. We will meet back here in three hours, remember to bring the mirror with you.

Narrator 1:   John takes the road towards the south and arrives to the palace. He knocks at the enormous door.

Guard 4:   What are you doing here?

John: Nothing.

Guard 4:   Are you sure?

John: I am sure.

Guard 4:   Ok.

John: I am just looking at your castle.

Guard 4:   Why?

John: 'Cause it is beautiful.

Guard 4:   Thank you.

John: You're welcome.

Guard 4:	You should look inside the castle, it is even more beautiful.
John:	For real?
Guard 4:	Yes.
John:	Thank you so much.

(Guard 4 and John enter the castle)

Narrator 2:	So John and the Guard enter the castle.
Narrator 1:	Meanwhile, Amy and Lisa get to the enchanted forest where Keisha and Mary are.
Amy:	Keisha, Mary, we came to get you.
Keisha:	Oh, thank goodness. We were really scared.
Lisa:	What happened?
Mary:	Keisha and I started fighting over the mirror and all of a sudden we were transported to Mirrorland. How did you get here?
Amy:	The boys got to the house and after talking a while we figured out that you had traveled to another dimension. Then Al told us that we could access a secret portal through an ice cream truck and here we are.
Keisha:	So where are the boys then?
Lisa:	Al and Rick went to find the Haunted Nurse to see if they could transform her again and help her cross back to our world. John went to spy on the Witch to make sure she is not following us.

Mary: We better hurry, the portal closes at midnight. If we don't get back home before that we will be stuck here forever.

Narrator 1: So the girls headed towards the castle hoping to find their friends on time.

Narrator 2: While the girls were walking through the forest and John was visiting the castle, Al and Rick ran into the Haunted Nurse. Unfortunately, the Haunted Nurse was not by herself.

Haunted Nurse: I want your spirit. Give it to me now!

Al: Ahhhh! Ruuuun!

Rick: Wow!

Witch: Seize those kids immediately!

Rick: Ahhh! I am too smart to die.

Al: Hmmm, don't witches die with water?

Rick: Oh yeah, I have some water, we can get the witch with it.

Al: Give me that.

(Rick and Al start fighting over the water until it spills on the floor)

Rick: Look what you did!

Al: Me? It wasn't me, I was just going to pour it on the witch.

Haunted Nurse: Now you have no way to run.

(She comes running on stage and slips on the puddle of water)

Witch: I will catch you.

(The Witch comes in and trips over the nurse falling to the floor)

Al: Well, water DID get them. *(laughs)*

Rick: Yeah.

Haunted Nurse: Get off me!

Witch: Don't think this is the end. You just ruined my hairdo, I
                 will never forgive you for that.

Al: We should have the mirror and show it to them.

Rick: Well, we don't have it.

Witch: Mirror? What mirror?

Al: The mirror that is the portal to our world.

Witch: I cannot look in any mirror, not with my hair like this.

Haunted Nurse: Do you have the mirror?

Rick: Yes, why?

Haunted Nurse: That is how I got into this world, that was a 100 years
                 ago. If I can transport myself back through the mirror I
                 will go back to my life.

Al: Well, I think we can help you go back.

Haunted Nurse: I will be eternally grateful if you did. Although to get back
                 to normal I would also have to eat a couple of chocolate
                 chip cookies.

Rick: *(taking the cookies out of his pocket)* Well, today is your
                 lucky day.

Witch: You cannot go! You are my best friend.

Haunted Nurse: Friend? You don't know the meaning of that word.

Witch: Fine. Leave me here.

Al and Rick: That is exactly what we plan to do.

Witch: Not if I can stop you.

Haunted Nurse: Well, you can't stop us. As soon as I step through the portal the curse you put on me will be lifted and I will go back to my normal life.

Rick: Come on Nurse, let's go.

Haunted Nurse: Thank you so much. Where are we going?

Al: We need to meet our friends. I think they all headed towards the castle.

Haunted Nurse: The castle? Did you also come to save the Queen?

Al and Rick: Queen? What queen?

Witch: You are talking too much!

Haunted Nurse: She locked the Queen in the tower of the castle a long time ago.

Witch: I said you are talking too much, I will have to destroy you immediately.

Haunted Nurse: Run.

Narrator 2: Al, Rick, and the Nurse ran towards the castle. The Witch ran after them but she was not as fast.

Narrator 1: At that very moment, John heard something coming from the tower.

Queen: Help! Help!

John: What is that?

Guard 4: Nothing, it is just the wind.

Queen: Help, help!

John: The wind doesn't yell for help!

Guard 4:	Fine, the Witch locked the Queen in the tower a long time ago. That is why the Witch rules the kingdom. Only someone from another dimension can free her.
John:	Well, as long as I am here, might as well.
Narrator 2:	John and the Guard climbed the 500 steps towards the tower.
John:	Queen, I came here to save you.
Queen:	Hurry, the Witch will be back soon.
John:	How do I get in?
Queen:	You will see some stairs by this old door.
John:	What door should I go in? There are too many.
Queen:	It is just an illusion. Choose the one in the middle, the yellow one.
John:	Here it is. Stand away from the door, I am going to push.
Queen:	Hurry up!
John:	It's stuck. I cannot do it by myself.
Queen:	Oh no, what are we going to do?
Guard 4:	I can help. We can push together. You just have to promise that you will destroy the witch.
John:	And how do I do that?
Guard 4:	You have to show her the reflection on a mirror.
John:	That's it?
Guard 4:	Yes, just one look at herself and she loses all her powers.

(from off stage)

Amy:	John, are you there?
John:	Yes, I am here, I am saving the Queen.
Keisha:	There is a Queen?
John:	I will explain later. Do you have the mirror with you?
Mary:	Yes, it's here.
John:	*(to the guard)* Okay, let's push the door together. One, two, three...
Queen:	Thank you, thank you so much.
John:	Hurry, let's go meet my friends downstairs.
Narrator 2:	The Queen, John and the Guard hurry downstairs where the girls were waiting for them.
Lisa:	I am so glad you are okay. Where are Rick and Al?

(Rick and Al come running in with the Nurse)

Rick:	Here we are. The Witch is after us.
Al:	We tried to run faster but we couldn't.

(Witch comes in)

Witch:	Now I see, all of you are here together. Queenie...how did you get out of the Tower?
Queen:	This nice boy and the Guard knocked down the door. I am free now.
Witch:	No, you are not. I will transform all of you into zebras.
Amy:	Zebras? Really?
Witch:	Yes, my favorite animal as it doesn't have any color.
Keisha:	You don't like blue?
Witch:	Oh no, I hate it.
Keisha:	What about pink?

Witch: Ugghhh! Horrible!

Keisha: No wonder you are so ugly.

Witch: How dare you? That is the last drop, you're out of luck...

John: Mary, take out the mirror!

Witch: The mirror?

Mary: The mirror that serves as a portal.

Witch: No!!! I can't look in the mirror.

Lisa: Well, I understand, your hair is pretty ugly.

Haunted Nurse: No, if she looks at herself she will turn into stone.

Lisa: Oh!!!

Queen: Fine, you don't have to look at yourself in the mirror but you have to leave the kingdom never to come back.

Al: As soon as we go back, the portal will close forever and you won't be able to trick anyone else to go through it again.

Rick: Anything you want from our world before we close the portal?

Witch: Coconuts.

Al and Rick: What????

Witch: That is the only thing I need from there. I cannot grow them here in Mirrorland.

Al: Fine, I will send a few over before destroying the portal.

Queen: Now leave. My soldiers will bring the coconuts to your cave and after that, we will never see you again.

Witch: Fine. *(she leaves)*

Queen:	Boys and girls, you have saved me and saved my kingdom. I have no way to thank you enough.
Rick:	Well, some ice cream would be nice.
Lisa:	Rick!
Rick:	What?
Haunted Nurse:	And you have saved me too. I will go through the portal first so I can go back to my life 100 years ago.
Queen:	After she leaves, you should cross the portal too. Please destroy the portal as soon as you get to your world. I will remember you fondly.
Narrator 2:	So the Nurse crosses de portal and goes back to her life.
Narrator 1:	After that, the children cross the portal one by one.
Amy:	Well, that certainly was an interesting adventure.
Lisa:	Tell me about it.
Rick:	I still have some cookies left in my pocket and they are delicious.

(He takes the cookies out and a photograph falls to the floor)

John:	What is that?
Rick:	What is what?
Al:	Something else fell out of your pocket.
Rick:	Oh this? It is an old photograph of my great grandmother when she was young. She was a nurse.
Keisha:	Let me see.
Mary:	Oh my god! Rick, your great grandmother was the nurse we saved in Mirrorland.

Amy: Well, this definitely was a night to remember. Nobody is going to believe us at school.

Narrator 1: And on that note, we reach the end of the story.

THE END

Confusion in the Castle

by 5th. grade students

Characters:

Detective 1 (ghost hunter)

Detective 2 (ghost hunter)

Melissa (teen girl)

Elizabeth (friend of the teen girl)

Brittany – 10 year old girl

Rachel – Stupid babysitter

Zombie (s)

Ghost (s)

Creepy Maid

Weird Ice Cream Man

Amy

Rosie

Abby

Samantha

(The Zombies and Ghosts are on stage just hanging around. They may be playing a game of cards or throwing a small ball at each other. A doorbell is heard. They looked at each other confused.)

(The Maid crosses the stage and opens the door.)

Maid: Can I help you?

Rachel: *(off stage)* I am sorry to bother you. My name is Rachel. I am their babysitter. Our car broke down the road and we need a place to stay for a few hours until someone can come get us. Do you mind if we came in?

Maid: Well, I am not authorized to let you in.

(She looks at the Zombies and Ghosts and they are signaling not to let them in.)

Rachel: Please, it is only me and three girls. I was taking them to the amusement park but we couldn't get there.

Maid: I really can't let you in.

(Brittany goes in front of Rachel.)

Brittany: *(off stage)* You are not being nice to us.

Maid: I am being as nice as I can.

Brittany: Well, I am tired and hungry and I need a place to rest.

(She passes the maid and gets to the middle of the living room)

(The Zombies and the ghosts hide behind the chairs/sofa.)

Maid: Well, aren't you something else!

Brittany: Actually I am perfectly adorable. *(she sticks her tongue out to her)*

(The zombies and ghosts sneak out from behind the couch.)

(Rachel, Melissa, and Elizabeth come in after her. Melissa and Elizabeth sit on the couch.)

Melissa:	*(texting)* He is not answering. Maybe there is no reception in this place.
Elizabeth:	Maybe he is upset that you didn't show up at the amusement park.
Melissa:	Do you think so?
Elizabeth:	Maybe he already found a new girlfriend over there. *(she laughs)*
Melissa:	That is not funny.
Rachel:	*(to the Maid)* Well, thank you for letting us come in, we won't be any trouble...
Maid:	You are trouble already...
Rachel:	I am sorry, I didn't know what else to do. I am new at babysitting, I didn't have an option.
Brittany:	Do you have something to drink?
Rachel:	Brittany, you don't ask if they don't offer you.
Brittany:	But I am thirsty.
Melissa:	Me too.
Elizabeth:	Me three.
Maid:	Sure, I will bring you lemonade that is to DIE for *(evil laugh)*. *(She exits)*
Melissa:	*(to Rachel)* Look where you brought us!
Rachel:	I know, I know, this is not the best place but I didn't have an option, besides, we are safe here.
Melissa:	If Rob breaks up with me it will be YOUR fault.

Brittany:	I am bored, I am going to see the rest of the house. *(she exits)*
Rachel:	Brittany, wait... *(she exits)*
Elizabeth:	Do you think your sister is safe with Rachel looking after her?
Melissa:	Probably not, we should go after them too.

(Elizabeth and Melissa exit. Maid comes in carrying a tray with a pitcher and glasses)

Maid:	Here is your...where did they go?

(There is a knock at the door. From offstage we can hear voices: Give me an O, give me a P, give me an E, give me an N...what does it say? Open, open. *Maid puts the tray down on a little table and goes to the door. She opens the door and the cheerleaders come in)*

Cheerleaders:	We are here, we are here, we finally arrived!
Maid:	Who are you?
Cheerleaders:	We are the greatest cheerleader squad!
Maid:	STOP!!!! Can't you just talk instead of cheering?
Cheerleaders:	We can try, we can try, yes we can!
Maid:	Stop, you are driving me crazy! *(She goes to the lemonade, pours herself a glass and drinks it. She spits out after the first gulp, remembering it is poisoned)*
Amy:	We are a group of cheerleaders...
Maid:	No???? Really? I wouldn't have guessed. Let me see, you got stranded and you are looking for a place to wait until your mom comes back from getting a mechanic.
Amy:	Actually, no...it was not our mom, it was the coach.

Rosie: You don't mind if we wait here, right?

Abby: Can I use your restroom? It was a long walk.

Samantha: Me too.

Maid: Sure, why not? Follow me. *(she exits)*

Amy: Oh no, we are not separating from each other, if you go,
              we go.

(All girls exit behind the Maid. Melissa and Elizabeth come back in)

Melissa: Did you hear something?

Elizabeth: Yes, it sounded like someone was yelling...almost like a
              cheer but that couldn't be.

Melissa: I am telling you, this place is haunted.

(Brittany comes running out of breath)

Brittany: Did you hear that?

Melissa & Elizabeth: Yes, we did.

Brittany: I think this place is haunted, isn't it awesome.

(Ghost 1 comes in without knowing the girls are there. He sees them and panics and runs back. Brittany sees him and points towards him)

Brittany: Did you see that?

Melissa & Elizabeth: Yes, we did.

Brittany: Let's go after it. *(she exits)*

(Cheers can be heard off stage)

Melissa: Elizabeth, I think there is more than one ghost...just
              listen.

(More cheers)

Elizabeth: I think you are right!

Melissa: We need to take care of Brittany, obviously Rachel

                can't.

Elizabeth: Okay, let's go.

(They exit. Cheerleaders enter. From the front we can see two detectives

hiding, listening to their conversation)

Amy: Well, that little excursion was interesting.

Rosie: This house is a little weird, isn't it?

Abby: Why do you say that? We only had to cross three

                hallways, five doors and go across two different foyers

                to get to the restroom.

Samantha: Yes, I almost didn't make it.

(From offstage - Melissa: *Brittney, where are you?,* Elizabeth: *Brittney,*

where are you?)

Rosie: Did you hear that?

Samantha: Give me a G, give me an H...

Amy: Stop that...we all know how to spell ghost.

Abby: I think this house is haunted.

All: *(huddling in the middle of the room)* Oh no!!!!

Amy: Maybe it was just the wind, let's go see where the noise

                came from.

(They exit)

Detective 1:   *(Climbing from the hiding place)* Okay, coast

                clear...come.

Detective 2:   Wassup?

Detective 1:   Excuse me?

Detective 2:   Sorry, what do you want?

Detective 1:   Well, did you bring the sound recorder?

Detective 2:   Yep.

Detective 1:   So...set it up behind the sofa!

Detective 2:   Okaaaaaay.

(Detective 2 sets the device behind the sofa)

Detective 1:   Now, come, let's set up the camera on the other room. We are going to prove once and for all that this place is full of ghosts.

Detective 2:   Sure, if you say so.

Detective 1:   Yes, I say so! I cannot see them or hear them...but I know they ARE here.

(Detective 2 shrugs.)

Detective 1:   Come on.

(Detective 2 starts stomping on the floor)

Detective 1:   Not like that! Softly...tip toe.

(Detective 2 exaggerates the moves and tip toes towards the side. They exit. Zombies enter from one side, Ghost 1 enters from another.)

Zombie 1:   Hey, what is going on?

Ghost 1:   I am not sure but all of a sudden our peaceful home has been transformed into a mad house. I haven't even been able to eat.

Zombie 1:   I hear ya. I am starving too.

Ghost 1:   Hey, we should go to Subway to get a Foot-long.

Zombie 2:   No, it would be better to go to Zomdonald's.

Ghost 1:   I don't like their Handburgers. Let's go to Papa Brains instead.

Zombie 2:	Zomdonald's!
Ghost 1:	Papa Brains!
Zombie 2:	Fine, but don't complain later that you didn't get enough meat.

(Ghost 2 enters dragging the pot.)

Zombie 1:	So, what is wrong with you?
Ghost 2:	I am really stressed out, I haven't been able to eat my soup today because some crazy girls keep on appearing everywhere...and they all scream with shrilling voices, I can't stand it.
Ghost 1:	Don't pay attention to them, you should be able to continue with your life....I mean, your death.
Ghost 2:	I can't, I can't. *(he starts crying)*
Zombie 1:	Breathe in, breathe out. We just have to manage to scare them enough so they stop bothering us.
Ghost 1:	And how do you suppose we do that?
Zombie 1:	Well, if we appear constantly besides them maybe they will get out of our way.
Ghost 1:	And maybe not...maybe they will start snooping around like those people so called detectives that the only thing they want to do us trap us.
Zombie 1:	We need help. You know what I mean, right?
Ghosts:	Yes, we believe we do...let's give him a call.

(They exit. Melissa and Elizabeth enter, they are fighting over the phone)

Rachel:	What is going on?
Melissa:	That is none of your business.

Rachel: Elizabeth?

Elizabeth: I can't tell, ask Melissa.

Rachel: Brittany?

(Britanny looks at both of them, checking if she should say something)

Rachel: Britanny?

Britanny: Well, Melissa was texting her boyfriend, but then
                 Elizabeth decided to start texting him too so they
                 started fighting over the cell phone. And then he got
                 upset so now he doesn't want to text or talk to Melissa
                 so she is upset.

(Clanking noise behind them. All of them freeze)

Melissa: Did you hear that?

Elizabeth: I did, did you?

Rachel: Stop changing the subject, there was nothing there.

(Noise again)

Rachel: I am sure that there is a perfectly logical explanation.

Britanny: Really? Like what?

Rachel: Well, mice...spiders...stuff...

All girls: Stuff?

Melissa: Stuff??? Sure, like stuff would make noise by itself.

(A ghost appears dragging a pot)

Rachel: Girls, get behind me immediately.

Britanny *(approaching the ghost)*: Who are you and why are you
                 dragging a pot?

Ghost: Boooooo....

Britanny: Boooo? I am sorry but if you don't speak I cannot
                understand you. *(she sticks her tongue at him)*

Melissa: Britanny, get away for him...that. Come on here.

Britanny: No, and you cannot make me!

(Melissa goes and grabs Britanny by the ear making her behind Rachel.
The Ghost goes across the stage just saying Booo and dragging the pot
behind him.)

Elizabeth: What was that?

Rachel: I am not sure but it seems to me it was a ghost.

The three girls: A ghost? Ahhhh!!!!

(They run off stage.)

Rachel: Yes, a ghost...a ghost? Ahhhhh!!!! *(She runs off stage)*

(Enter Detective 1 and 2)

Detective 1:   According to our investigation most of the paranormal
                activity in this house happens here in the living room.

Detective 2:   Yep.

Detective 1:   And according to our recordings from yesterday night,
                there were a lot of unexplained

noises that occurred here between midnight and one   o'clock in
the morning.

Detective 2:   Yep.

Detective 1:   *(a little annoyed)* And according to what people have
                said that is the time where they have seen shadows at
                the windows.

Detective 2:   Yep.

Detective 1:   Is there something you would like to add?

Detective 2:   Nope.

Detective 1:   Sometimes I wonder why I keep working with you.

(Detective 2 shrugs. Maid enters.)

Maid: Can I offer you something to drink?

(Detective 2 hides behind Detective 1)

Detective 1:   Well, what do you have available?

Maid: Oh, we have some lemonade that is do DIE for! *(evil laugh)*

Detective 1:   Anything else?

Maid: Well, yes, the usual, coffee, tea, water...boooooring!!!!

Detective 1:   I will have coffee, no sugar, no cream...black.

Maid: *(to Detective 2)* And you Sir?

Detective 2:   Nothing.

Maid: Are you sure? It seems that it is going to be a dark, long night. *(evil laugh)*

Detective 2:   Yep. Sure

Maid: Very well then. *(exits)*

Detective 1:   Well, that was kind of creepy.

Detective 2:   Yep.

Detective 1:   Oh geez! *(exits)*

(Detective 2 watches him go and then exits the other way. Cheerleading can be heard from the outside of the living room. The cheerleaders enter chanting a cheer).

Rosie: So where the heck are we?

Amy:	Yeah, great idea girls...oh, let's not wait in the bus any more for the coach to come back, let's get help ourselves.
Samantha:	I told you it was a bad idea but nooooo...you got all excited and started jumping up and down.
Abby:	Just because you never want to do anything doesn't mean that we shouldn't.
Samantha:	Don't use that tone with me, after all, I am not the leader of the group...obviously, I wasn't qualified enough.
Aby:	I told you I didn't want to be the leader, the coach said I should.
Samantha:	Whatever...
Aby:	Don't whatever me...
Rosie:	Girls, girls, stop!!!! We are in enough trouble already.
Amy:	Give me an S, give me T, give me an O, give me a P....what does it spell: STOP, STOP...
Rosie:	You stop too!!!!

(Maid appears)

Maid:	Good evening.

(All girls turn around)

Amy:	Hi, we are kind of lost.
Maid:	Yes????
Amy:	Well, we are wondering if you could help us.
Maid:	Maybe.

Samantha: Let me handle this. (*to the Maid*) Look, we just came from the road, our van broke and we were on our way to a cheerleading contest and if we don't get there on time then we will be disqualified and we won't be able to go to the high school we want.

Maid: Ok. (*she turns around and leaves*)

Amy: Samantha! You scared her!

Rosie: Now we will not get ANY help at all. (*starts sobbing*)

(*Ice Cream man enters but the girls do not see him, they only see a floating tray with ice creams behind*)

Abby: (*picking up one of the ice creams from the tray and licking it*) Thank you, this is delicious.

(*All the other girls look at the floating tray with a distraught look*)

Abby: What? Want to try?

Samantha: (*whispering*) Look behind you.

(*Abby turns around and freezes, in front of her is the floating ice cream tray. She puts the ice cream on the tray and they all exit*)

Girls: Ahhhh!!!!

Ice cream man: Well, that was easy...after all, I still got the talent. I hope my friends are happy with this. After this, I am sure that the girls will leave and the house will be quiet and peaceful again.

Detective 2:   Finally I got rid of the other detective. He could be so annoying thinking he is always right. Now, where should I start? The first noise I heard was this way...

(Ice cream man appears. He gets really close to Detective 2, positioning himself right at her back. Detective 2 turns around and sees him.)

Detective 2:   Well, so what are you doing here with that ice cream?

(Ice Cream man freaks out)

Ice Cream man: Can you see me?

Detective 2:   Of course I can see you.

Ice Cream Man: But nobody is supposed to see me.

Detective 2:   Why?

Ice Cream man: Well, I am a….ghost. Not just any ghost…a terrifying ghost.

Detective 2:   Yeah, I can see that.

Ice Cream man: And nobody is supposed to see me.

Detective 2:   Oh…I am a psychic…I see everything.

Ice Cream Man *(terrified)*: Please, don't hurt me, don't hurt me.

Detective 2:   Chill…how could I hurt you? You are already dead.

Ice Cream Man: *(smiling)* Oh yeah, that's right.

(Zombie 2 appears.)

Zombie 2:   *(whispering)* hey man, what are you doing talking to that guy?

Ice Cream Man: *(whispering back)* He can see me.

Zombie 2:   Oh.

Detective 2:   And I can understand you too.

Zombie 2:   What????

Detective 2:   Yep.

Zombie 2:   *(whispering)* What are we going to do now?

Detective 2:   I can still heeeear youuuu.

Zombie 2:   Right. So?

(Ice Cream Man shrugs.)

Detective 2:   So, I have a plan. Call your other friends the ghosts and the zombies and we can talk.

Detective 1:   *(offstage)* Where are you?

Detective 2:   Oh no! Here he comes again. Okay you two, go and call your friends, I will get rid of him.

(Ice Cream Man and Zombie 2 exit.)

Detective 2:   In the living room.

(Detective 1 comes in)

Detective 1:   Where were you? I have been looking all over for you? Have you been here all the time?

Detective 2:   Yep.

Detective 1:   Just follow me, don't separate.

Detective 2:   Nope.

(They exit. Ghost 2 enters)

Ghost 2:   *(yelling)* Zombies, where are you? Ghost? Zombies?

(Zombie 1 appears)

Zombie 1:   Shhh...don't yell.

Ghost 2:   *(whispering)* Why not?

Zombie 1:   The house is full of people and I don't want them to hear us.

Ghost 2:   Oh, right.

Zombie 1:   What do you want?

Ghost 2:   I just wanted to know if you found Ice Cream Man.

Zombie 1:   I did, I asked him to scare everyone away, he is the only one that could do it.

(Ice Cream Man comes running)

Ice Cream Man: Guys... I am glad I found you. Where are the other two?

Ghost 2:   They would be back from Papa Brains in no time.

(Ghost 1 and Zombie 2 enter carrying a pizza box)

Ghost 1:   Here it is. Hot and steamy.

Zombie 2:   Hot and steamy like my brains.

(All of them look at him annoyed)

Ice Cream Man: Stop, pay attention. There is a Detective here that can see us because he is also a psychic. He will come here as soon as he gets rid of the other Detective Lady.

(Maid appears)

Ice Cream Man: Where were you? We have been looking all over for you?

Maid: I have been hiding from the intruders...all these girls think it is my responsibility to serve them just because I am a Maid...go figure!

Ice Cream Man: I know...all of us are upset. The Detective has a plan.

(Detective 2 comes in)

Detective 2:   I see that everyone has gathered here already. So here is the deal, I can help you get rid of the intruders.

Maid: Really?

Ghost 1:   Wait...what do you want as exchange?

Detective 2:   In exchange, I will be able to come here any time I want so I can write a book about ghosts and zombies.

Ice Cream man: Hold on, we have to talk.

(All of them get into a huddle)

Ice Cream Man: Okay, we agree. The only day you cannot come here is Halloween though, that is our private celebration.

Detective 2:   Fine. This is what you need to do. The Zombies will scare the girls that are with the babysitter and they will guide them to the living room. At the same time, the Ghosts will scare the cheerleaders and guide them to the living room. The point is for both parties to get here together at the same time and then they will think that the other party was making the noise and things move.

Zombie 2:   Wow! Great idea!

Ghost 2:   I guess we can try.

Maid: Okay, then, what are you waiting for?

(Ghosts and Zombies exit. Detective 1 enters)

Maid: Here he comes again.

Detective 1:   Where were you?

Detective 2:   Right here.

Detective 1:   Why didn't you wait for me?

Detective 2:   Enough! Just chill. I am tired of you pushing me around. I already talked to the Ghosts and Zombies, they are pretty nice actually.

Detective 1:   You what? You talked to them without me?

Detective 2:   Yep.

Detective 1: This is unbelievable, we have investigating this haunted house for years now...I can't handle this. (*He leaves*)

Detective 2: Good riddance! Now, to work. (*to the Maid*) You stay here, wait for everyone to come back.

Maid: Okay.

(*Detective 2 exits. From one side of the stage the girls and babysitter appear running and screaming. From the other side the cheerleaders appear doing the same. Confusion on stage*)

Brittany: Who are you?

Rachel: Brittany, we don't talk to strangers!

Amy: Relax, we are cheerleaders that got stranded on the road.

Melissa: The same happened to us, we were on our way to the amusement park.

Abby: You were? That is where we were heading. We are enrolled in a cheerleading competition over there.

Elizabeth: Really? We were on our way to see you. Melissa and I love cheerleading.

Rosie: Wow! Maybe you could be part of the squad.

Melissa: That would be great. *(cell phone rings)* Michael? Oh my god! I thought you were upset with me!...really? ...oh great...see you soon.

Elizabeth: What did he say?

Melissa: He is not upset, his battery died. He said he found out where we are as the coach of the cheerleader squad got to the amusement park. They are heading here to pick us up.

Cheerleaders: We are getting out of here, we are getting out of here!

Brittany: Wait! Aren't we forgetting this house is haunted?

Rosie: Oh yes. We heard voices calling for Brittany.

Rachel: We heard voices cheering.

All of them pointing to the other ones: It was you! *(they all laugh)*

Amy: Then this house is not haunted.

Elizabeth: Let's get to the road so they can pick us up from there.

Cheerleaders: Yeah, let's go!

(All exit. The Maid goes to the door and watches them leave)

Maid: Everyone! Coast is clear!

(Ghosts, Zombies, and Ice Cream Man come out)

Ghost 2:   I thought they were never going to leave.

Ice Cream Man: Finally some peace and quiet.

Ghost 1:   Yeah, let's order something at Papa Brains.

Zombie 2:   Zomdonalds!

Zombie 1:   Oh no, here we go again!

(Detective 2 comes out)

Detective 2:   I can see this is the beginning of an excellent partnership.

THE END

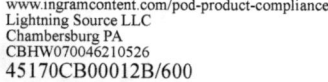